SIMON AND SCHUSTER BOOKS FOR YOUNG READERS
Simon & Schuster Building, Rockefeller Center
1230 Avenue of the Americas, New York, New York 10020

Copyright © 1991 by Jerome Martin

All rights reserved including the right of
reproduction in whole or in part in any form.
SIMON AND SCHUSTER BOOKS FOR YOUNG READERS
is a trademark of Simon & Schuster Inc.

Designed by Vicki Kalajian

Manufactured in Singapore

10   9   8   7   6   5   4   3   2   1

ISBN: 0-671-69556-8

Note: The concept, text and illustrations for *Mitten/Kitten*
are the work of Jerome Martin. With the author's
permission, the illustrations for this edition
have been redone by Daniel Collins based on
Jerome Martin's originals.

Produced by CONCEPTS PUBLISHING, INC.

BOMC offers recordings and compact discs, cassettes
and records. For information and catalog write to
BOMR, Camp Hill, PA 17012.

mitten/kitten

By Jerome Martin

SIMON AND SCHUSTER BOOKS FOR YOUNG READERS
Published by Simon & Schuster Inc.
New York / London / Toronto / Sydney / Tokyo / Singapore

m kitten

m.onkey

judge

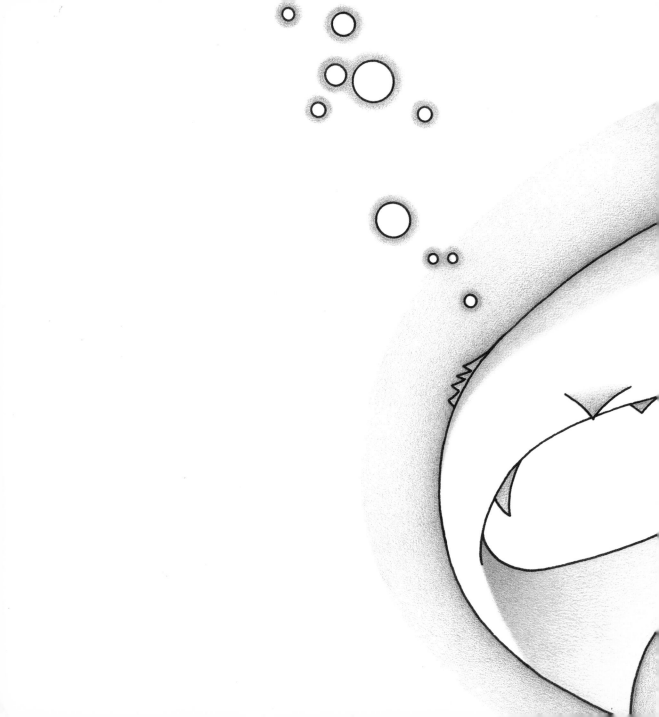

sh

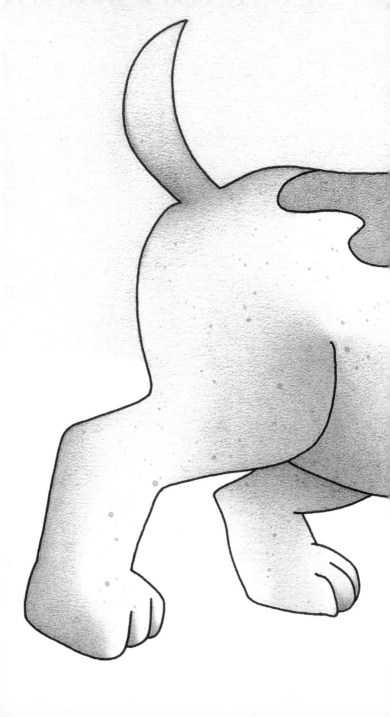

bark

cr own

spider

f **ork**

sleep

Motherhood

22 21 20 19 18   5 4 3 2 1

Text © 2018 Gibbs Smith Publisher

Illustrations © 2018 Sarah Cray

Published by
Gibbs Smith
P.O. Box 667
Layton, Utah 84041

1.800.835.4993 orders

www.gibbs-smith.com

Gibbs Smith books are printed on paper produced from sustainable PEFC-certified forest/controlled wood source. Learn more at www.pefc.org.

Printed and bound in Hong Kong

Library of Congress Control Number: 2017947922

ISBN: 978-1-4236-4798-0

Motherhood

55 REFLECTIONS ON WHAT IT MEANS TO BE A MOM

ILLUSTRATED BY SARAH CRAY

GIBBS SMITH
TO ENRICH AND INSPIRE HUMANKIND

FOR ELLA & LUNA,

MY WILDFLOWERS.

Mothers are the gardeners of the human Race.

ANNA A. ROGERS

You go through big chunks of time where you're just thinking, "This is impossible — oh, this is impossible." And then you just keep going, and you sort of do the impossible.

TINA FEY

To describe my mother would be to write about a hurricane in its perfect power. Or the climbing, falling colors of a rainbow.

MAYA ANGELOU

Sometimes the
of motherhood

natural

strength
is greater than
laws.

BARBARA KINGSOLVER

Motherhood has a very humanizing effect. Everything gets reduced to essentials.

MERYL STREEP

Motherhood is the most challenging as well as the utmost satisfying vocation in this world.

NITA AMBANI

ONE THING I HAD LEARNED FROM
WATCHING CHIMPANZEES WITH THEIR
INFANTS IS THAT HAVING A CHILD
SHOULD BE FUN.

Jane Goodall

Our mothers always remain the strangest, craziest people we've ever met.

MARGUERITE DURAS

The human heart was not designed to beat outside the human body, and yet, each child represented just that — a parent's heart bared, beating forever outside its chest.

DEBRA GINSBERG

Grown don't mean
nothing to a mother.
A child is a child.
They get bigger, older,
but grown?...In my heart
it don't mean a thing.

TONI MORRISON, BELOVED

Moms
are like buttons:
They hold everything
together.

ALL THAT I
AM, OR HOPE
TO BE, I OWE
TO MY ANGEL
MOTHER.

ABRAHAM LINCOLN

BEING A MOTHER IS AN ATTITUDE NOT A BIOLOGICAL RELATION

ROBERT A. HEINLEIN

Some are kissing mothers and some are scolding mothers, but it is love just the same, and most mothers kiss and scold together.

PEARL S. BUCK

the
heart
child's

Mother's is the Schoolroom.

HENRY WARD BEECHER

Mothers
hold our tiny
hands just for
a while, but
they hold our
hearts forever.

there is a
special sweetness
in being able to
participate in
Creation.

PAMELA S. NADAV

Mothers and their category all their own. strong in the entire instantaneous and

children are in a

There's no bond so

world. No love so

forgiving.

GAIL TSUKIYAMA

The older
the more
Mom was

I get,
I realize
right.

sweater, n.:

GARMENT WORN BY A CHILD
WHEN ITS MOTHER IS FEELING
CHILLY.

AMBROSE BIERCE

The danger of motherhood: You relive your early self, through the eyes of your mother.

JOYCE CAROL OATES, THE GRAVEDIGGER'S DAUGHTER

Home
is where
mom is.

The moment a child is born She never existed before, mother, never. A mother is

the mother is also born.
the woman existed, but the
something absolutely new.

RAJNEESH

This is what we do, my mother's life said. We find ourselves in the sacrifices we make.

CAMMIE MCGOVERN,
NEIGHBORHOOD WATCH

because of her,

i am me.

a mother's heart
is a special place
where her children
are always home.

Nothing is lost until your mother can't find it.

that best
academy,
a mother's
knee.

JAMES RUSSELL
LOWELL

An ounce of mother is worth a pound of clergy.

RUDYARD KIPLING

the raising of a child is the building of a cathedral. you can't cut corners.

DAVE EGGERS, A HOLOGRAM FOR THE KING

MOTHER

All love begins

HOOD:

and ends there.

ROBERT BROWNING

She never quite leaves her children at home, even when she doesn't take them along.

MARGARET CULKIN BANNING

The natural state of motherhood is unselfishness. When you become a mother, you are no longer the center of your own universe. You relinquish the position to your children.

JESSICA LANGE

I will look after you and after anybody you be looked after, any here. I brought my I am

I will look
say needs to
way you say. I am
whole self to you.
your mother.

MAYA ANGELOU, MOM & ME & MOM

I am sure that
if the mothers of
various nations could
meet, there would be
no more wars.

E. M. FORSTER

If evolution really works, how come mothers only have two hands?

MILTON BERLE

A worried mother does better research than the FBI

If you're completely exhausted and don't know how you're going to keep giving this much of yourself day after day, you're probably a good parent.

BUNMI LADITAN

there's no way
to be a perfect
mother, and a
million ways to
be a good one.

JILL CHURCHILL

Once you sign on to be a mother, that's the only shift they offer.

JODI PICOULT, MY SISTER'S KEEPER

Hundreds of dewdrops
to greet the dawn,
Hundreds of bees
in the purple clover,
Hundreds of butterflies
on the lawn,
But only one mother
the wide world over.

GEORGE COOPER

Being a mother
is not about what you
gave up to have a child, but
what you've gained from
having one.

good moms have messy kitchens, laundry piles, sticky floors, and happy kids.

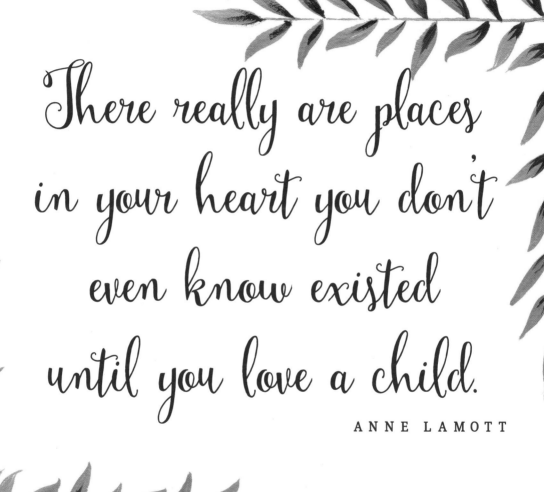

There really are places
in your heart you don't
even know existed
until you love a child.

ANNE LAMOTT

The art of motherhood involves much silent unobtrusive self-denial, an hourly devotion which finds no detail too minute.

HONORÉ DE BALZAC

Yes, Mother. I can see you are flawed. You have not hidden it. That is your greatest gift to me.

ALICE WALKER

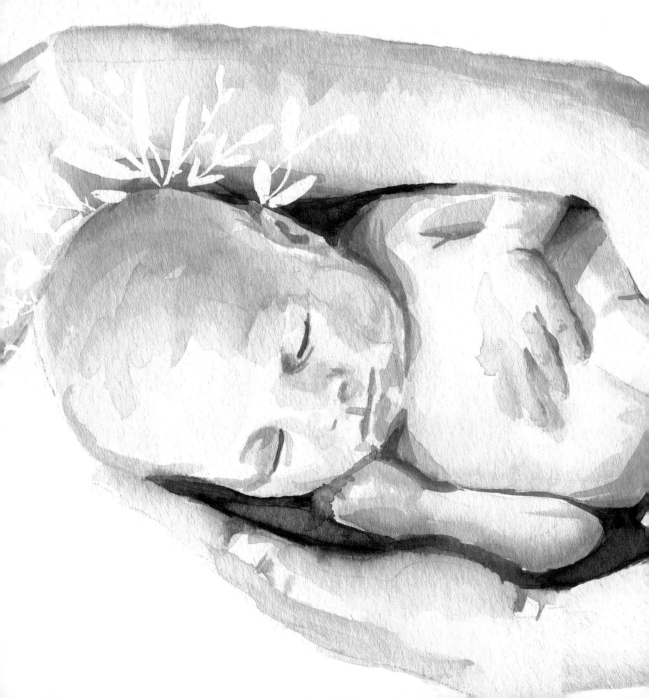

A MOTHER'S

ARMS ARE

MADE OF

TENDERNESS

AND CHILDREN

SLEEP SOUNDLY

IN THEM.

Victor Hugo

Motherhood is the greatest thing and the hardest thing.

RICKI LAKE

MOTHERHOOD
IS A KIND
OF WILDERNESS
THROUGH WHICH EACH
WOMAN HACKS
HER WAY,
PART MARTYR,
PART PIONEER...

Rachel Cusk

Mother is a verb,

not a noun.

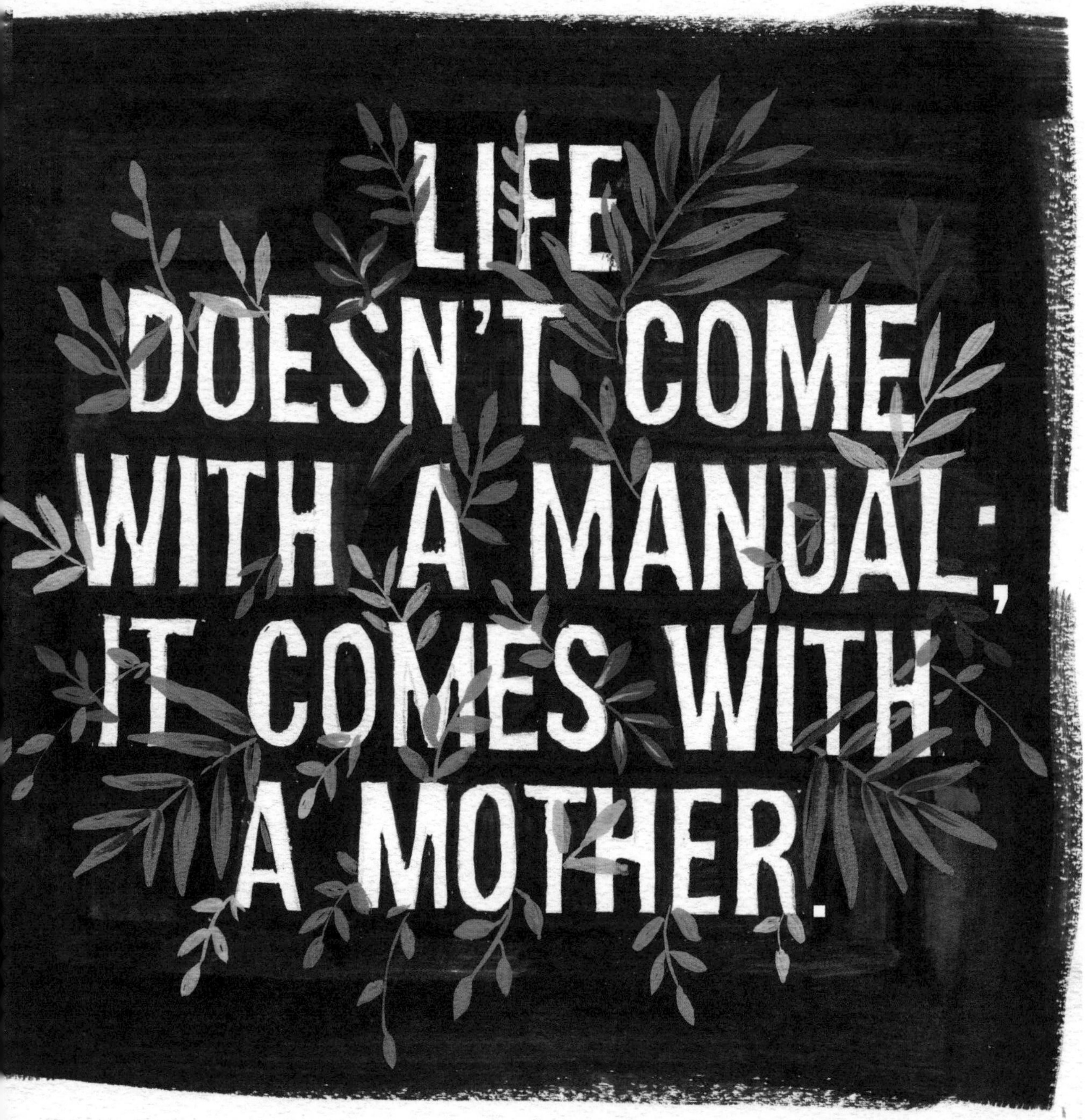
LIFE
DOESN'T COME
WITH A MANUAL;
IT COMES WITH
A MOTHER.

Whatever else
this stinking
world, a mother's

is unsure in
dunghill of a
love is not.

JAMES JOYCE

God could not
be everywhere
and therefore he
made mothers.

You know you're a mom when you understand why Mama Bear's porridge was cold.

however motherhood comes to you, it is a miracle.

SHERYL CROW

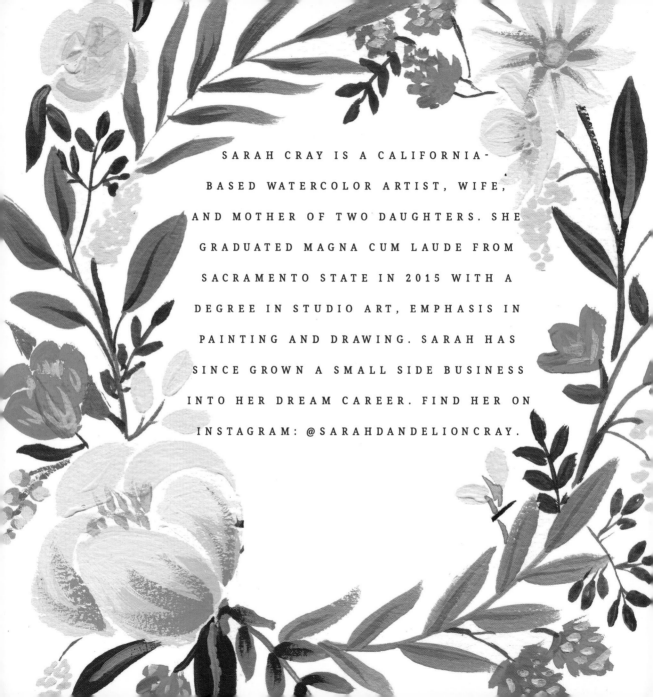

SARAH CRAY IS A CALIFORNIA-BASED WATERCOLOR ARTIST, WIFE, AND MOTHER OF TWO DAUGHTERS. SHE GRADUATED MAGNA CUM LAUDE FROM SACRAMENTO STATE IN 2015 WITH A DEGREE IN STUDIO ART, EMPHASIS IN PAINTING AND DRAWING. SARAH HAS SINCE GROWN A SMALL SIDE BUSINESS INTO HER DREAM CAREER. FIND HER ON INSTAGRAM: @SARAHDANDELIONCRAY.